Fabled Catharsis

Samantha Teves

BookLeaf
Publishing

Presentation by *BookLeaf Publishing*

Web: www.bookleafpub.com

E-mail: info@bookleafpub.com

ISBN: 9789358369038

First edition 2023

DEDICATION

For River,

you are forever my greatest inspiration.

PREFACE

I wrote this collection of poems to lend a space to those kindred spirits who feel life so deeply and live it with their hearts on their sleeves. It's a collection inspired by the human experience, the unimaginable, the magical, the beautiful, the intricacies of it all, the catharsis we all seek.

Cheers, to this simply awe-inspiring thing that is our lives.

Ghosts in the Trees

I've been whispering my secrets to the trees for
as long as I can remember
dripping tears into brambles, joys spilt across
gnarled roots
Listeners of the grandest order, patient and wise
mutes
I wonder how many sorrows, how many secrets
they bury every November

Centuries of fractured hearts, frayed pride, and
stolen kisses under the boughs
Roots planted; a menagerie of lives projected in
translucent layers onto this place
Lover's trysts, a life laid to rest, blood spilled, a
mother's soft embrace
The forest holds time, lives imprinted on the
wood, voices speaking ancient vows

I will pour my heart here, crimson and beating
unabashedly against the dirt
Perhaps they will hold my story too, a memory
content among the ghosts
Woven into the leaves, blooming in spring,
where my story can boast

I will whisper my very soul to the trees,
whispering the peace, the hurt

Spell Hope

Raindrops on pink sneakers. Sweet steam from a laundry vent. The broken blind that shows a sliver of blue sky. Sweaters with sleeves that cover hands. A loved one's muffled voice from another room. The color green. A blanket balled up at the foot of a bed. Coffee that's too hot. Smile lines. The special fork that reminds you of childhood. The smell of gardenia. The voicemail in the saved folder. Orchestral theme songs. Nostalgic bumper stickers. Triple texts. The smell left on a pillow. The number 3. Art deco lampshades. Hand-painted picture frames. Wet patio furniture. Toenail polish. Bookmarks. Vacuum lines on carpet. Initials drawn on steamed mirrors. The color yellow. Summer dresses. Faded scars. The flicker of a candle. Thunder. Forehead kisses. The way the light changes at sunset. Songs that make you cry. Tea bags at the bottom of cups. A letter long forgotten.

Golden

There is a golden line
It weaves in soft swivels through a road dappled
green

Golden like warm wheat beyond the fences
Like the fabled apple of myth
Golden like lips across a shoulder blade
Like streetlights pooling on fresh snow

There is a golden line
In longing gazes, blue and green meeting for the
first time

Golden like the Sun's breath on bare lower
backs
Like the days could never fade
Golden like champagne dripping from fogged
flutes
Like the softest whisper hitting just behind your
ear

There is a golden line
Living, breathing, watching, in those
earth-colored eyes

Something

Something is calling me
A siren's haunting high note
A spun, silvery, twine pulled across seas
A hand, dry and rough, a cliff washed in moss
There is something out there

A life that I'll never see
A shelter that would hold me close
Woolen sweaters and wet grass knees
A silhouette of onyx curls, a flame through the
dark
There is something out there

There is a life unlived
A love unanswered
A story never to be told
My heart beating in a place I'll never know

Water Sun, Earth Moon

Am I made of water, am I made of earth?

dripping heart, dirty toes,

a moon bathed in green

love letters and rings buried behind the shed

a boat full of holes

am I made of stars, am I made of soil?

unyielding, incorrigible

a sky washed with purple

wishes unreturned on dandelion wings

am I made of raindrops, am I made of clay?

Cardinal

Jagged and crimson
A flame built of sand
Scales that shift
Hearts that mend

A moon written on, red lace font
A love song to the where I am going and the
who I have been

Orange and pulsing
Sparks guiding lips
Warmth inhaled, gulping

Armored, silk skin below
A moment of calm before the reckoning, a battle
to be won

Wordless

He follows in a colorblind chariot
Wheels leaving no silhouette
Wordless in his somber pursuit

Shape of night, edgeless and eternal
Hand reaching, smug lips beseeching
Wordless in his resolve

Death rides so peacefully
No stir, no commotion, a soft song sung
Wordless in his eternity

Courted, for an entire life long
A raven vanguard, perched on a fencepost
Wordless in his persistence

Drop it

Set it down

The heart tattered blue
The weight of their words
The worry of eyes that pry

Set it all down

The judgement of the expected
The mind worn weary
The standards not met

Set them down

The unkindnesses
The way you thought it would be
The past that holds fast

Set it all down
Drop it
Leave it here on this floor
Set it down
Set it down
Set it all down

Mother

One day, much sooner than I would like
I will be the one looking up to your face
Your hand will dwarf mine
Your embrace will place my head on your
shoulder
Your little laugh will deepen
Your eyes will lose that youthful softness

But for this day, my love
You are my wonder
You are the sunshine
You are my heart set free to walk and play on
this Earth

When one day does come, and come it surely
will
I will remember these days
When you reached for my hand to help you
climb
To steady you as you gaze the possibilities of
this world

When one day comes
My hand will still be here
Always

Wrap it in Green

Read the books with green covers
they've many secrets inside
Stories of lovers and sinners
Tears to be cried

Green when your heart feels spilled
The wash of leaves and moss
Green writes the folklore fables
The staggering stories of loss

The hue that teaches
The truth about living and whim
Think of a more honest color
Closed eyes, into green you swim

Fairytale

Forever in fairytales, in worlds of misbelief
wrapped in peachy tulle, blushed heart on her
sleeve
worlds that hold whimsy and strange, not to fear
Forever sprawling on toadstools with unseen
humming songs in her ear

A world that cannot be broken with maturation
painted with rose and smeared streaks of gold
bare toes on woven carpets, rolled out in
charming indecision
Forever wandering will-less woods, lensed in
passionfruit vision

Don't open the eyes, dear girl, nestle down into
the floral
clover-woven ankle chains and silver thistle
crowns
a shelter in this sugared place, so peculiar
Forever fairytale, a far off place, no passing
thought for tomorrow

Blue

It's blue
oceans and summer skies, to wax cliche
but blue can also wash in sordid shame
it's the unbreakable bond, it's me and you

It was blue
that she loved about you, coaxed her in
so safe, soft comforts, wisdoms written in
cerulean ink
and now, only a red-rimmed strangeness

It was blue
the thing they loved in me
that manic reflection, innocent, wide and too
welcoming
upward eyelash gaze, once, the only thing I
could love too

It's blue
quivering with anger, white, water-logged
misgivings
it's blue that keeps me tethered, no matter how
far I pull
He was blue, so are you, and now it lives inside
me too

Forgotten

Show me,
the spaces inside that time forgot to touch
the callused, the silenced, the scorned

Show me,
where the dust has settled, where you drape your
winter jackets
where the fingers can't reach to ease the itch

Show me,
the damp, the black and blue
the spaces hollowed out, cavities dug to the bone

Show me,
all the places time has left no mark
nothing mended, no washed and well

Show me
where it bleeds
where it burns

Show me
Invite me
Let me

Meet You There

Will you remember, do you?
The life that was once laid bare at your
summer-blushed toes
Trees alive, singing to the lovers in
lavender-drenched smoke
Naked Luna, silver sweat, watching without
judgement

Will you share the memory, have you?
Fields overgrown, overhead, dancing reeds and
fireflies in frenzy
Sunset melting into sorbet kisses, pop beats
under foggy heads
A dreamscape that is forever etched in, but never
to be found again

Have you told the tale, was I mentioned?
Too many voices, floating on the empty, infinite
space
Blonde over bare knees, and seats reconfigured
for long legs
Daring, vernal games, nerves heedless of danger

Do you visit, from time to time?

The places where breath melted onto the green
paths, dew and lust
The headlights, gold on silver-lit skin, eyes red,
dripping, dream-soaked
I will meet you there, in the jurassic summer
fields, where love learned our names

Humankind

17

Will it ever be enough?

Time has soaked my pink shoes and it's not
something easily washed out
Will it ever be soft?

Reality has left it's tattered pages all over the
bedroom
Will it ever stop?

Violence seeped red into the walls, and the stains
sing me to sleep
Will it ever be enough?

Hypothesis has barricaded the flowered cottage
gates, and all we can do is watch
Will it ever be soft?

I'm disenchanted with the glass I pick from the
rose petals
Will it ever stop?

There are souls on the sidewalk, and everyone
just moves around them
Will it ever be enough?

Humankind, I am begging you

Lion

Red is the lion's kiss
Soul pulled through parted lips, willing
surrender
Gulped, hungry, waiting

Red is the fang
Pressed, bone into flesh, exposed
Piercing, thirsting, needing

Red is lace on the floor
Claws, hipbones, a carved love letter
Weaving, breathing, biding

Red, scarlet lines woven up a vertebrae ladder
Dehydrated rose petals, held fast in clenched
teeth
Dreaming, chilling, pouring

Found It

I found it/Right there, in the place where your lashes meet your face/In the way your hands move with your lips/In the softness of your voice when it says my name/I found it/ On the tattoo laid against your heart/ In the bones beneath your skin/ In the way your smile at the shadows/ I found it/ Sitting softly in the scar on your knuckles/Tucked into the curl when your hair gets too long/ In the way your eyes soften when you see someones heart/ I found it/ Home.

Madonna

Am I the swan

Am I the crow

Laces, leathers and subtlety, I don't know

Am I the silhouette

Am I the shadow

Bare skin stung pink by purple dead nettles

Am I the kiss

Am I the snake

Repulsed by the pleasures, we refused to take

Am I the soft

Am I the raw

Poison seeped in, fade to black, I know what he saw

Lavender

lavender laid across her lap, the sea's noise
holding it fast
a heather reminder of the before and after
sorrow, beading into delicate knots, dripping
from tired fingertips

I won't cry for you

english tea stained and torn notebook paper, I
will write it to forget
purple flowers, dried upside down on rusted
nails
nostalgia isn't welcome here anymore, windows
open, raining

I won't cry for you

Scream

open your mouth
like a snake, unhinged and gaping
open wide to the gods watching
scream

open your lungs
there is no apology here, violent
open to the seas churning
scream

open your chest
spill your secrets, dripping, throbbing, burning
open to the eavesdropping pines
scream

open your arms
spine flexed, bones twisting rigid in wrath
open to the rocks, moss climbing, dripping
scream

scream

scream

Moon Dance

wind on bare feet that cross the dark moors
moon mother watching in silent reverence
they move to the wood's sable song

roses with black thorns, dropped one by one to
flame
ink sky sparkling with maybes
the shadowed specters will answer this
enchantment

they call the maiden, perhaps the mother too
bellies cast orange by fire's glow
here, she will do her witches waltz

writhing, spines bending, lips parted
feet that aren't bound to the earth
a feral call to the wilds, a promise asked and
answered

bone and blood, bare hips in the forest
hands dance, weaving hypnotic patterns
words whispered eaten by the darkest sky, an
incantation, a charm, a wish